1·2·3 MURALS

Written by Jean Warren

Illustrated by Cora L. Walker

Simple Murals To Make
From Children's Open-Ended Art

Totline
PUBLICATIONS

Warren Publishing House
A Division of Frank Schaffer Publications
Torrance, California

Editor: Gayle Bittinger
Contributing Editor: Elizabeth S. McKinnon
Assistant Editor: Claudia G. Reid
Layout and Cover Design: Kathy Jones
Cover Illustration: Marion Hopping Ekberg

ISBN 0-911019-22-7

Library of Congress Catalog Card Number 89-050121
Printed in the United States of America
Published by: Warren Publishing House

Editorial Office: P.O. Box 2250
                    Everett, WA 98203
Business Office: 23740 Hawthorne Blvd.
                    Torrance, CA 90505

Introduction

1•2•3 MURALS is filled with ideas for making eye-catching seasonal bulletin boards with child-created materials. Cooperation comes naturally as your children work together to create these delightful displays in which each child's art work is valued as a part of the whole.

Every mural includes directions for an open-ended art activity and instructions for putting it all together to complete a scene. Several of the murals have patterns to accompany them. We encourage you to adapt the patterns and the murals to meet your individual needs and to use materials you have on hand.

You will find that fostering your children's creativity and encouraging cooperation is fun and easy with the ideas in **1•2•3 MURALS.**

Contents

Murals

Contents

Murals *Continued*

Borders

Mural Patterns

Murals

Happy Faces Mural

Materials: Hand mirror; paper plates; butcher paper; construction paper; felt-tip markers; yarn; glue; pair of scissors.

Preparation: Cut small circles out of construction paper for eyes and cut yarn into hair-length pieces. Hang butcher paper on a wall or a bulletin board.

Activity: Give each child a paper plate. Have the children take turns looking at themselves in a hand mirror. Ask them to notice the colors of their hair and eyes. Then let them make self-portraits by gluing yarn "hair" and construction paper "eyes" that match their own hair and eye colors on their paper plates. Have the children complete their self-portraits by adding noses and mouths with felt-tip markers.

Mural: Attach the self-portraits to the butcher paper and write the children's names below them. Add the words "Welcome, Happy Faces" to the mural.

Susan M. Paprocki
Northbrook, IL

Clown Mural

Materials: Paper plates; butcher paper; tempera paints; paint brushes; felt-tip markers; yarn; pair of scissors.

Preparation: Use felt-tip markers to draw a clown figure on butcher paper. Hang the butcher paper on a wall or a bulletin board.

Activity: Give the children paper plates. Let them use tempera paints and paint brushes to turn their paper plates into colorful balloons.

Mural: Attach a piece of yarn to each balloon plate, then attach the plates to the butcher paper. Gather all the yarn pieces together and fasten them to the clown's hand.

Dinosaur Swampland Mural

Materials: Blue butcher paper; dark green or brown butcher paper or posterboard; green construction paper; scissors.

Preparation: Hang blue butcher paper on a wall or a bulletin board. Cut three to four large dinosaur shapes out of dark green or brown butcher paper or posterboard. Then cut a 9- by 12-inch sheet of green construction paper in half lengthwise for each child.

Activity: Give each child one of the green construction paper rectangles. Have the children use scissors to cut slits along one of the long sides of their rectangles to make grass strips. Then give them each a second rectangle. Help them round off the ends of these rectangles before letting them cut all around their rectangles to make fern shapes.

Mural: Attach the fern and grass shapes to the butcher paper. Position the dinosaurs on the mural to look like they are grazing, walking or standing in the swamp.

Autumn Leaves Mural

Materials: White typing paper; watercolor paints; butcher paper; brown tempera paint; paint brushes; pair of scissors.

Preparation: Paint a large brown tree with bare branches on butcher paper. Hang the paper on a wall or a bulletin board.

Activity: Let the children paint sheets of white typing paper with watercolor paints. Encourage them to use autumn leaf colors such as red, yellow, orange and brown. When the paint has dried, use the patterns on pages 60 and 61 as guides to cut leaf shapes out of the papers.

Mural: Attach the leaf shapes to the butcher paper, some on the tree branches and some beneath the tree. If desired, cut squirrel and nut shapes out of construction paper and add them to the mural.

School Bus Mural

Materials: Photo of each child; white construction paper; yellow tempera paint; paint brushes; black felt-tip marker; tape; glue; pair of scissors.

Preparation: Use the patterns on pages 62 and 64 as guides to cut the front and back of a school bus shape out of white construction paper. Use the pattern on page 63 as a guide to cut out one middle section of the bus shape for every two children. Tape the sections together and place them on a table.

Activity: Let the children work together to paint the school bus shape yellow. Allow the paint to dry.

Mural: Outline the wheels and windows and draw other details on the bus shape with a black felt-tip marker. Cut out the windows and glue a photo of one child in each window opening. Hang the school bus mural on a wall at the children's eye level.

Columbus Day Mural

Materials: White cloth; blue butcher paper; blue and brown construction paper; glue; pair of scissors.

Preparation: Use the pattern on page 65 as a guide to cut three ship shapes out of brown construction paper. Make sails for the ships by cutting white cloth into sail shapes. Hang blue butcher paper on a wall or a bulletin board and attach the ship and sail shapes to the paper. Cut 1- by 8-inch strips out of blue construction paper. Set out the paper strips and glue.

Activity: Show the children how to fasten the ends of the strips together with glue to make paper chains. Then let them make their own chains with as many loops as they wish.

Mural: Attach the paper chains in wavy lines underneath the ships on the butcher paper to make an ocean.

Pumpkin Patch Mural

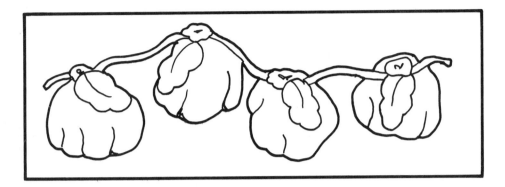

Materials: Small paper bags; newspapers; green twist ties; brown butcher paper; green construction paper; orange and green tempera paint; paint brushes; green yarn; tape; pair of scissors.

Preparation: Use the pattern on page 66 as a guide to cut pumpkin leaf shapes out of green construction paper. Attach a long piece of brown butcher paper to a wall at the children's eye level.

Activity: Give each child a small paper bag. Have the children stuff their bags with crumpled pieces of newspaper. Secure each bag with a green twist tie, leaving about 1 inch gathered at the top. Then let the children paint the bottom parts of their bags orange and the top parts green to create pumpkins with stems.

Mural: String the pumpkins together with a long piece of green yarn and attach them to the butcher paper. Tape the green leaves on the pumpkin stems and the green yarn "vine."

Turkeys in the Barnyard Mural

Materials: Butcher paper; brown and red tempera paints; paint brushes; black felt-tip markers; construction paper; pair of scissors.

Preparation: Cut a large barn shape, a fence shape and other barnyard shapes out of construction paper. Glue the shapes on the butcher paper to create a barnyard scene. Place the butcher paper on a table.

Activity: Let the children make turkey handprints all over the barnyard scene. Have them paint their fingers and palms brown and their thumbs red. Then have them press their hands, painted sides down, on the butcher paper, leaving "turkey" prints. After the paint dries, let the children add eyes, beaks, legs and feet to their turkey prints with black felt-tip markers.

Mural: Hang the barnyard mural on a wall or a bulletin board.

Turkey Feathers Mural

Materials: Feathers; brown butcher paper; construction paper; tempera paints; shallow containers; pair of scissors.

Preparation: Cut a large turkey shape out of brown butcher paper and hang it on a wall or a bulletin board. Cut large turkey feather shapes out of construction paper. Pour several colors of tempera paint into shallow containers.

Activity: Give the children the feather shapes and feathers. Let them use their feathers as brushes to paint designs on their feather shapes.

Mural: Attach the painted feather shapes to the turkey shape.

Thanksgiving Quilt Mural

Materials: Aluminum foil; scraps of colorful paper; construction paper; tape; glue; pair of scissors.

Preparation: Cut 9-inch squares out of construction paper. Crease the squares diagonally both ways. Cut diamond shapes out of colorful paper and aluminum foil.

Activity: Give each child one of the creased squares. Let the children glue the diamond shapes on their squares in patterns. Show them how to use the creases on their squares as guidelines.

Mural: Arrange the squares in a rectangular shape on the floor and tape them all together. Carefully hang the paper quilt on a wall or a bulletin board.

Karel Kilimnik
Philadelphia, PA

Thanksgiving Dinner Mural

Materials: Large paper tablecloth; paper plates; magazines; construction paper; glue; pair of scissors.

Preparation: Cut a cornucopia shape and several different fruit shapes out of construction paper. Glue them to the center of a paper tablecloth.

Activity: Let the children look through magazines to find pictures of foods. Have them tear out the pictures and glue them on paper plates.

Mural: Attach the paper plates around the edges of the tablecloth. If desired, let the children glue plastic forks, knives and spoons next to the plates. Then hang the tablecloth on a wall or a bulletin board.

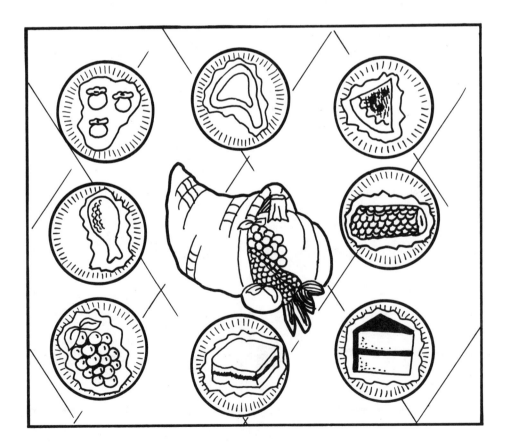

Log Cabin Mural

Materials: Dowel; brown paper bags; butcher paper; tape; glue; pair of scissors.

Preparation: Cut the bottom flaps off of brown paper bags. Roll each bag lengthwise around a dowel. Secure with tape to keep the bag from unrolling, then take the dowel out. Continue this procedure to make as many "logs" as desired. Place butcher paper on a table or on the floor.

Activity: Give the children the paper bag logs. Let them work together to glue the logs in a log cabin shape on the butcher paper.

Mural: Hang the mural on a wall or a bulletin board. Add tree shapes and a chimney shape cut out of construction paper, if desired.

Hanukkah Mural

Materials: Gold glitter; blue butcher paper; cotton swabs; yarn; Popsicle sticks; glue; shallow containers; pair of scissors.

Preparation: Hang blue butcher paper on a wall or a bulletin board. Cut out yellow construction paper letters to spell "Happy Hanukkah" and attach them to the top of the butcher paper. Pour small amounts of glue into shallow containers.

Activity: Give each child six Popsicle sticks. Have the children use cotton swabs to cover their Popsicle sticks with glue. Then let them sprinkle gold glitter over the glue. Have them wait a few moments before shaking off the excess glitter. Show each child how to glue his or her Popsicle sticks together to make two triangles. Allow the glue to dry. Then help each child glue his or her triangles together to make a Star of David.

Mural: Attach each child's Star of David to the butcher paper.

Popcorn Wreath Mural

Materials: Popped popcorn; ribbon; posterboard; butcher paper; glue; shallow containers; pair of scissors.

Preparation: Cut a large wreath shape out of posterboard. Hang butcher paper on a wall or a bulletin board. Use a piece of ribbon to make a bow. Pour small amounts of glue into shallow containers.

Activity: Have the children dip pieces of popped popcorn into the glue and place them all over the wreath shape. Let them continue until the wreath is completely covered with popcorn.

Mural: Add the bow to the top of the popcorn wreath and attach the wreath to the butcher paper.

Christmas Wreath Mural

Materials: Pencils; butcher paper; red and green construction paper; glue; scissors.

Preparation: Hang butcher paper on a wall or a bulletin board. Cut a bow shape out of red construction paper.

Activity: Give the children pieces of green construction paper and pencils. Help the children use the pencils to trace around their hands on the construction paper. Let them cut out their hand shapes.

Mural: Overlap the hand shapes in a circle on the butcher paper to make a wreath. Glue the bow shape to the bottom of the wreath.

Tree of Hands Mural

Materials: Aluminum foil; pencils; butcher paper; green construction paper; felt-tip markers; scissors.

Preparation: Hang butcher paper on a wall or a bulletin board. Use felt-tip markers to write the words "Happy Holidays" at the top. Cut a large star shape out of aluminum foil.

Activity: Give the children pieces of green construction paper and pencils. Help the children use the pencils to trace around their hands on the construction paper. Let them cut out their hand shapes.

Mural: Use the hand shapes to make a large Christmas tree shape on the butcher paper. Starting at the bottom, overlap the hands in progressively shorter rows with the fingers pointing down. Decorate the tree by attaching the large foil star at the top.

Extension: Make presents to put under your tree by having the children fold pieces of foil wrapping paper around small squares and rectangles cut out of cardboard. Let them decorate the presents with self-stick bows. Attach the presents to the mural.

Triangle Tree Mural

Materials: Foil cupcake liners; assortment of stickers, fabric and felt scraps, beads, buttons, glitter and sequins; butcher paper; green construction paper; glue; pair of scissors.

Preparation: Cut 12- by 12- by 12-inch triangles out of green construction paper. (You will need a total of four, nine, or sixteen triangles to complete a tree.) Hang butcher paper on a wall or a bulletin board.

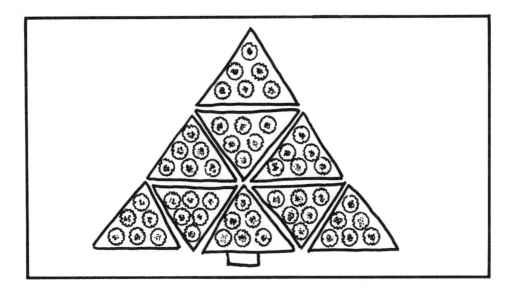

Activity: Give each child a triangle and six foil cupcake liners. Have the children flatten their liners and glue them, shiny sides up, on their triangles. Let the children decorate their triangles with stickers, fabric and felt scraps, beads, buttons, glitter or sequins.

Mural: Attach the decorated triangles in a tree shape on the butcher paper. If you have four triangles, place three on the bottom (alternating point up, point down), then place the fourth triangle on the top, point up. If you have nine triangles, alternate five triangles on the bottom, three on the second row and one on top. If you have sixteen triangles, alternate seven triangles on the bottom, five on the second row, three on the third row and one on top. Use felt-tip markers to add a star, a tree trunk and several Christmas packages to the mural, if desired.

Toy Train Mural

Materials: Magazines and toy catalogs; butcher paper; construction paper; glue; pair of scissors.

Preparation: Use the patterns on pages 67 and 69 as guides to cut an engine shape and a caboose shape out of construction paper. Then use the pattern on page 68 as a guide to cut out a construction paper boxcar shape for each child. Hang a long piece of butcher paper on a wall at the children's eye level.

Activity: Let the children look through magazines and toy catalogs and tear out pictures of their favorite toys. Give them each a boxcar shape and have them glue on their toy pictures.

Mural: Attach the engine shape, all of the boxcar shapes and the caboose shape to the butcher paper to complete the mural.

Ornament Mural

Materials: Glitter; butcher paper; construction paper; cotton swabs; green felt-tip marker; tape; glue; shallow containers; pair of scissors.

Preparation: Use the patterns on pages 70 and 71 as guides to cut ornament shapes out of construction paper. Hang a long piece of butcher paper on a wall at the children's eye level. Use a green felt-tip marker to draw evergreen branches across the top part of the butcher paper. Pour small amounts of glue into shallow containers.

Activity: Give the children the ornament shapes. Let them dip cotton swabs into the glue and use them to make designs on their shapes. Then have the children sprinkle glitter all over the glue. Have them wait a few seconds before shaking off the excess glitter.

Mural: Let the children help tape the ornaments to the evergreen branches on the butcher paper.

Snow Pal Mural

Materials: Cotton balls; white butcher paper; construction paper; glue; shallow containers; pair of scissors.

Preparation: Cut two large circles out of white butcher paper, making one slightly smaller than the other. Place the circles on a table. Pour small amounts of glue into shallow containers. Set out the containers and cotton balls.

Activity: Let the children dip the cotton balls into the glue and place them all over the circles. Have them continue until the circles are completely covered with cotton balls.

Mural: Put the Snow Pal Mural together by attaching the circles to a wall or a bulletin board with the larger circle on the bottom. Then decorate the snow pal with facial features and clothing shapes cut out of construction paper.

Snowscene Mural

Materials: Cotton balls; blue or black butcher paper; construction paper; glue; shallow containers; pair of scissors.

Preparation: Cut a house shape out of construction paper and glue it on blue or black butcher paper. Pour small amounts of glue into shallow containers. Place the butcher paper on a table.

Activity: Let the children dip cotton balls into the glue and place them all over the butcher paper for snowflakes. Show the children how to fluff out some of the cotton balls and glue them in front of the house shape to make a snowy lawn.

Mural: Hang the mural on a wall or a bulletin board.

Winter Forest Mural

Materials: Aluminum foil; Ivory Snow powder; water; small bowls; spoon; light blue butcher paper; green construction paper; paint brushes; pair of scissors.

Preparation: Hang light blue butcher paper on a wall or a bulletin board. Cut a pond shape out of aluminum foil and attach it to the center of the paper. Use the pattern on page 72 as a guide to cut tree shapes out of green construction paper. In small bowls stir Ivory Snow powder with water until the mixture is thick and creamy.

Activity: Give each child a tree shape and a paint brush. Let the children brush the Ivory Snow mixture over their tree shapes to create a snowy look. Allow the shapes to dry.

Mural: Attach the snow-covered trees around the pond shape on the butcher paper to create a winter scene.

Dot to Dot Mural

Materials: Self-stick circles; crayons; butcher paper.

Preparation: Hang a long piece of butcher paper on a wall at the children's eye level.

Activity: Give each child several self-stick circles. Let the children place their circles all over the butcher paper.

Mural: Have the children use crayons to draw lines from "dot to dot" to complete the mural.

Valentine Heart Mural

Materials: Red posterboard; butcher paper; red, pink and white construction paper; felt-tip marker; glue; pair of scissors.

Preparation: Cut a large heart shape out of red posterboard and cut it into puzzle pieces (one for each child). Mark the back side of each puzzle piece with a felt-tip marker.

Activity: Give each child a puzzle piece and sheets of red, pink and white construction paper. Let the children tear their construction paper into small pieces. Have them place their puzzle pieces on a table with the marked sides facing down. Then let them glue their torn-up papers all over their puzzle pieces.

Mural: Help the children assemble and glue the heart puzzle on a piece of butcher paper. Hang the heart puzzle on a wall or a bulletin board.

Queen of Hearts Mural

Materials: Post-it brand 3- by 3-inch note pad; old deck of playing cards; butcher paper; construction paper; felt-tip markers; glue; pair of scissors.

Preparation: Separate the cards in the heart suit from the rest of the cards in a deck of playing cards. Cut sheets of a 3- by 3-inch Post-it brand note pad into fourths so that part of the sticky strip is on each piece. Then cut small hearts out of construction paper. Hang a long piece of butcher paper on a wall at the children's eye level. Cut more hearts out of construction paper to make a simple "Queen of Hearts" as shown above. Attach the Queen of Hearts to the butcher paper.

Activity: Give each child four pieces of the Post-it brand note pad strips, a heart playing card and a small paper heart. Let the children arrange their strips on their cards like arms and legs. To complete their heart people, have them glue their paper hearts to the tops of their cards for heads and add faces with felt-tip markers.

Mural: Attach the heart people to the butcher paper in rows next to the Queen of Hearts.

Brick Building Mural

Materials: Butcher paper; red construction paper; glue; scissors.

Preparation: Fold pieces of red construction paper in thirds. Hang butcher paper on a wall at the children's eye level.

Activity: Give each child a piece of the folded construction paper. Have the children cut their papers along the folds to create construction paper "bricks."

Mural: Let the children work together gluing bricks to the butcher paper to build a structure such as a house, a fort or a wall.

Pot of Gold Mural

Materials: Black posterboard; butcher paper; red, orange, yellow, green, blue and purple construction paper; tape; pair of scissors.

Preparation: Cut red, orange, yellow, green, blue and purple construction paper into 1- by 8-inch strips. Hang butcher paper on a wall or a bulletin board. Cut a pot shape out of black posterboard and attach it to one side of the butcher paper.

Activity: Show the children how to tape the ends of the construction paper strips together to make paper chains. Then have each child select paper strips of one color and make a chain with them.

Mural: Attach the paper chains to the butcher paper to make a rainbow shape that ends in the "pot of gold." Add a construction paper leprechaun shape and shamrock shapes to the mural, if desired.

Shamrock Puzzle Mural

Materials: Posterboard; butcher paper; various shades of green construction paper or tissue paper; cotton swabs; felt-tip marker; glue; shallow containers; pair of scissors.

Preparation: Cut a large shamrock shape out of posterboard. Cut the shape into puzzle pieces (one for each child). Mark the back side of each puzzle piece with a felt-tip marker. Cut green construction paper or tissue paper into small squares. Pour small amounts of glue into shallow containers.

Activity: Let the children use cotton swabs to spread glue over the unmarked sides of their puzzle pieces. Then have them cover the glue with squares of green paper to create mosaic designs.

Mural: Help the children put the shamrock puzzle together and glue it on a piece of butcher paper. Then hang the shamrock mural on a wall or a bulletin board.

March Kites Mural

Materials: Eye droppers; cotton balls; blue butcher paper; construction paper; tempera paints; yarn; glue; pair of scissors.

Preparation: Cut kite shapes out of construction paper. Fold each shape in half lengthwise. Hang blue butcher paper on a wall or a bulletin board. Fluff out several cotton balls and glue them on the butcher paper for clouds.

Activity: Give each child a kite shape. Let the children unfold their shapes and use eye droppers to squeeze drops of tempera paint on one side of their papers. Then have them refold their shapes and rub their hands gently across the tops. Let them open up their kite shapes to reveal the designs they have made. Attach pieces of yarn to the shapes for kite strings.

Mural: Attach the kite shapes to the butcher paper "sky." If desired, add construction paper bird shapes to the mural.

Night Sky Mural

Materials: Posterboard; aluminum foil; dark blue or black butcher paper; yellow construction paper; pair of scissors.

Preparation: Use the pattern on page 73 as a guide to cut star shapes out of posterboard. Tear aluminum foil into 16-inch sheets. Hang dark blue or black butcher paper on a wall or a bulletin board.

Activity: Set out the star shapes and the sheets of foil. Let the children carefully wrap the foil around the stars.

Mural: Attach the foil-covered stars to the butcher paper. Add a yellow construction paper moon shape to complete the night sky scene.

Easter Parade Mural

Materials: Decorating materials such as ribbon, rickrack, feathers, buttons, stickers and sequins; butcher paper; white and yellow construction paper; glue; pair of scissors.

Preparation: Use the patterns on pages 74 and 75 as guides to cut a bunny body shape and two bunny ear shapes for each child out of white construction paper. Then use the hat pattern on page 75 as a guide to cut brimmed hat shapes out of yellow construction paper. Hang a long piece of butcher paper on a wall at the children's eye level.

Activity: Give each child a bunny body shape, two bunny ear shapes and a hat shape. Have the children glue their bunny ears and their hat shapes to their bunny bodies. Then let them decorate their hats by gluing on such materials as straw flowers, ribbon, rickrack, feathers, buttons, stickers and sequins.

Mural: Attach the bunnies to the butcher paper to create an "Easter Parade."

Easter Egg Mural

Materials: Evaporated milk; food coloring; muffin tin; Easter grass; brown posterboard, burlap or corduroy; butcher paper; white construction paper or typing paper; paint brushes; pair of scissors.

Preparation: Mix evaporated milk with drops of food coloring in the cups of a muffin tin. Hang butcher paper on a wall or a bulletin board. Cut a large basket shape out of brown posterboard, burlap or corduroy and attach it to the butcher paper.

Activity: Give each child a piece of white construction paper or typing paper. Have the children use paint brushes to paint designs on their papers with the colored milk. Let the papers dry for six to eight hours before cutting them into egg shapes.

Mural: Attach the egg shapes in and around the basket shape on the butcher paper. Add some Easter grass to the top of the basket.

Bunny Trail Mural

Materials: Cotton balls; butcher paper; white and green construction paper; butcher paper; felt-tip markers; glue; scissors.

Preparation: Use the pattern on page 76 as a guide to cut bunny shapes out of white construction paper. Cut sheets of green construction paper in half lengthwise. Cut egg shapes out of white construction paper. Attach a long piece of butcher paper to a wall at the children's eye level.

Activity: Give each child a bunny shape, a half sheet of green construction paper and several egg shapes. Have the children cut slits along one of the long sides of their green construction paper pieces to make grass strips. Then have them glue cotton ball tails on their bunny shapes and decorate their egg shapes with felt-tip markers.

Mural: Help the children glue their grass strips to the butcher paper to create a trail. Then let them glue their bunny shapes all along the grass trail and their egg shapes beside the trail.

Rainy Day Mural

Materials: Butcher paper; construction paper; tempera paints; paint brushes; pair of scissors.

Preparation: Cut umbrella shapes out of construction paper. Hang butcher paper on a wall or a bulletin board.

Activity: On a rainy day, give each child an umbrella shape. Let the children use tempera paints and paint brushes to create designs on their shapes. While the paint is still wet, have them put on their raincoats, go outside and hold their shapes in the rain for a short time. Then have them bring their shapes back inside and talk about the designs created by the rain.

Mural: Attach the umbrella shapes to the butcher paper. Add construction paper handles and raindrop shapes.

Spring Garden Mural

Materials: Yellow, pink and green cupcake liners; pipe cleaners; light blue butcher paper; yellow and green construction paper; glue; scissors.

Preparation: Hang a long piece of light blue butcher paper on a wall at the children's eye level. Glue green construction paper strips across the bottom of the paper for flower stems. Use the pattern on page 77 as a guide to cut daffodil shapes out of yellow construction paper.

Activity: Set out the daffodil shapes and yellow, pink and green cupcake liners. Let each child make a daffodil by gluing a yellow cupcake liner to a daffodil shape. Then have the children flatten the green cupcake liners and cut them in half to use for leaves. To make butterflies, have the children pinch together the middles of pink cupcake liners. Then help them twist pipe cleaners around the middles and curl the ends of the pipe cleaners to make antennae.

Mural: Let the children glue their daffodil shapes and green leaves to the stems on the butcher paper. Then attach their butterflies either to the tops of their flowers or to the blue sky background.

Caterpillar Mural

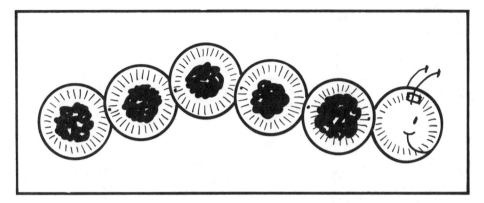

Materials: Sponges; paper plates; brass paper fasteners; pipe cleaners; butcher paper; tempera paint; felt-tip markers; shallow containers; pair of scissors.

Preparation: Pour small amounts of tempera paint into shallow containers. Cut sponges into squares. Hang a long piece of butcher paper on a wall at the children's eye level.

Activity: Give each child a paper plate and a sponge square. Let the children dip their sponges into the paint, then press them on their paper plates. Allow the paint to dry.

Mural: Hook the plates together in a row with brass paper fasteners. Add a plate with a caterpillar face drawn on it and two pipe cleaner antennae. Attach the paper plate caterpillar to the butcher paper, arranging the plates so that the caterpillar appears to be moving.

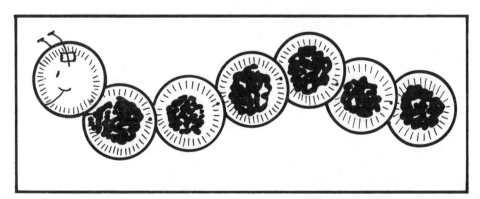

Nosegay Mural

Materials: Large and small paper doilies; flower stickers; blue butcher paper; pair of scissors.

Preparation: Hang blue butcher paper on a wall or a bulletin board. Cut large paper doilies in half and attach the halves to the butcher paper in a large circle.

Activity: Give each child a small doily and several flower stickers. Let the children attach their stickers to their doilies any way they wish.

Mural: Attach the sticker-covered doilies to the butcher paper in the middle of the doily circle to complete the nosegay.

Dragon Mural

Materials: Aluminum foil; textured object; butcher paper; green, yellow and blue construction paper; glue; pair of scissors.

Preparation: Hang butcher paper on a wall or a bulletin board. Cut a large dragon shape out of butcher paper. Cut scale shapes out of aluminum foil and green, blue and yellow construction paper.

Activity: Give the children the foil scale shapes. Let them make textures on the foil by placing the shapes on a textured object and gently rubbing across them with their hands. Then have the children glue the foil scales and the construction paper scales all over the dragon shape.

Mural: Attach the dragon shape to the butcher paper. Use felt-tip markers to add a castle and other background details, if desired.

Sunflower Mural

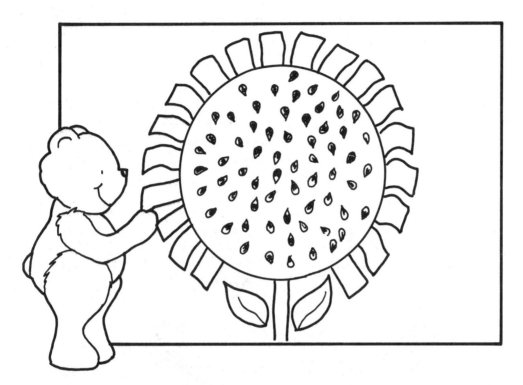

Materials: Yellow crepe paper; unshelled sunflower seeds; butcher paper; yellow and green construction paper; tape; glue; shallow containers; pair of scissors.

Preparation: Tape pieces of yellow construction paper together and cut a large circle out of them. Pour small amounts of glue into shallow containers. Hang butcher paper on a wall or a bulletin board. Cut yellow crepe paper into 2- by 6-inch strips.

Activity: Place the large circle on a table along with the containers of glue, the crepe paper strips and unshelled sunflower seeds. Have the children glue the crepe paper strips around the edge of the circle to make petals. Then let them dip the seeds into the glue and place them all over the circle.

Mural: Attach the sunflower to the butcher paper. Add a green construction paper stem and leaf shapes.

Teddy Bears' Picnic Mural

Materials: Magazines; rinsed and dried coffee grounds; small paper plates; brown, red and white construction paper; cotton swabs; glue; shallow containers; pair of scissors.

Preparation: Use the pattern on page 78 as a guide to cut a bear shape for each child out of brown construction paper. Cut small pictures of foods out of magazines. Make a large checkered tablecloth out of sheets of red and white construction paper and attach it to a wall or a bulletin board. Pour small amounts of glue into shallow containers.

Activity: Give the children the bear shapes. Have them use cotton swabs to cover their shapes with a thin layer of glue and let them sprinkle rinsed and dried coffee grounds all over the glue. Set the bear shapes aside to dry. Give each child a small paper plate. Let the children glue "lunch goodies" on their paper plates using the precut pictures of foods.

Mural: Attach the bear shapes and the paper plates to the tablecloth. If desired, add a picnic basket cut out of construction paper.

Ants at the Picnic Mural

Materials: Magazines; paper tablecloth; small paper plates; stamp pads; glue; pair of scissors.

Preparation: Cut pictures of foods out of magazines. Spread a paper tablecloth on a table.

Activity: Give each child a paper plate to glue to the tablecloth. Then have the children glue the precut food pictures on the plates. Let them add "ants" to the mural by lightly touching their thumbs to stamp pads and pressing their thumbs on the tablecloth.

Mural: Hang the tablecloth on a wall or a bulletin board.

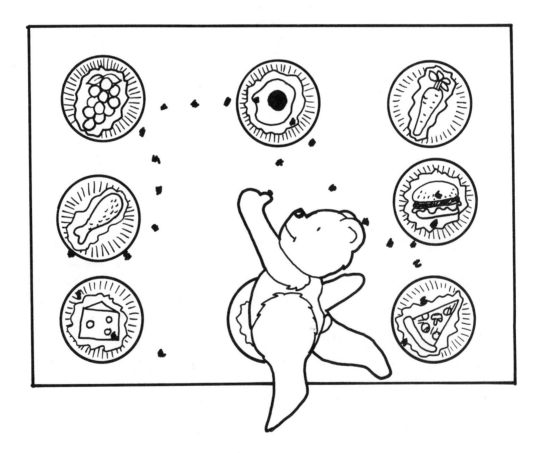

Nature Mural

Materials: Fish net; small paper bags.

Preparation: Set out the fish net and give the children small paper bags.

Activity: Go on a walk with the children. Let them use their paper bags to collect nature objects such as feathers, flowers, leaves and grasses. When you return, let the children weave their nature objects through the holes in the fish net. Encourage them to weave items horizontally, vertically and diagonally.

Mural: Hang the net on a wall or a bulletin board. Continue to add nature objects as the children find them.

Fireworks Mural

Materials: Dish scrubbers; black butcher paper; tempera paints; shallow containers.

Preparation: Pour small amounts of tempera paints into shallow containers. Place black butcher paper on a table along with the paint containers and dish scrubbers.

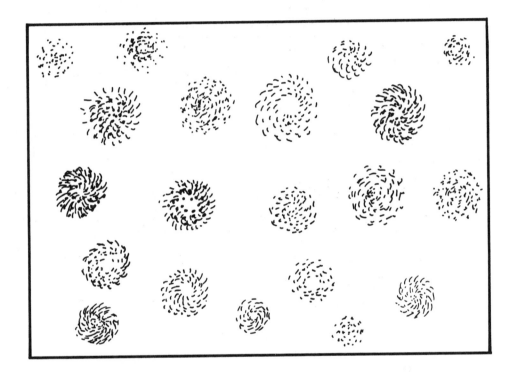

Activity: Have the children dip the scrubbers into the paints and lightly touch them to the butcher paper to make "fireworks" prints. Let them continue until the black "sky" is filled with exploding fireworks.

Mural: Hang the mural on a wall or a bulletin board.

Variation: Let the children print fireworks on pieces of black construction paper. Tape the papers together and hang them on a wall or a bulletin board.

Flag Mural

Materials: Brightly colored vinyl tape; self-stick circles in various colors; butcher paper; construction paper; pair of scissors.

Preparation: Hang butcher paper on a wall or a bulletin board. Cut brightly colored vinyl tape into a variety of lengths. Set out the tape strips and self-stick circles.

Activity: Give each child a piece of construction paper. Let the children attach the tape pieces and self-stick circles to their papers any way they wish.

Mural: Hang the flags in columns on the butcher paper. Add long strips of tape for flagpoles, if desired.

Footprints in the Sand Mural

Materials: Pencil; butcher paper; light brown construction paper; blue and brown tempera paints; paint brushes; glue; scissors.

Preparation: Place a long piece of butcher paper on the floor. Use a pencil to draw a line lengthwise down the middle of the paper.

Activity: Let the children work together to paint the top half of the butcher paper blue (for the sky) and the bottom half of the paper brown (for the sand). Set the paper aside to dry. Have the children take off their shoes and stand on pieces of light brown construction paper. Use a pencil to trace around their feet and let them cut out their footprints. If desired, have the children brush glue on their footprints and sprinkle them with sand.

Mural: Let the children glue their footprints on the brown half of the butcher paper to make footprints in the sand. Attach the butcher paper to a wall at the children's eye level. If desired, add other shapes cut out of construction paper, such as a sun, a pail, a shovel, a beach ball and a beach umbrella.

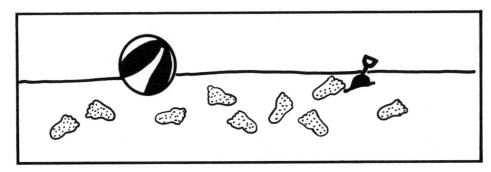

Borders

Polka Dot Border

Materials: Self-stick circles; black construction paper; pair of scissors.

Preparation: Cut sheets of black construction paper in half lengthwise to make 4½- by 12-inch strips.

Activity: Give each child a strip of construction paper and several self-stick circles. Let the children place the circles on their papers any way they wish.

Border: Attach the strips along the edges of a bulletin board to create a polka dot border.

Winter Border

Materials: Cotton balls; light blue construction paper; glue; shallow containers; pair of scissors.

Preparation: Cut sheets of light blue construction paper in half lengthwise as shown above to create a scalloped effect. Pour small amounts of glue into shallow containers. Set out cotton balls and the containers of glue.

Activity: Give the children the scalloped pieces of construction paper. Show them how to gently fluff out the cotton balls. Then have them dip the cotton balls into the glue and place them on their papers.

Border: Attach the construction paper pieces, scalloped sides facing in, around the edges of a bulletin board.

Valentine's Day Border

Materials: Paper doilies; construction paper; felt-tip markers; glue; pair of scissors.

Preparation: Cut construction paper into heart shapes small enough to fit on the paper doilies.

Activity: Give the children the heart shapes. Let them decorate their shapes with felt-tip markers. Then have each child glue his or her decorated heart to the center of a doily.

Border: Attach the doilies around the edges of a bulletin board to create a valentine border.

Variation: Instead of heart shapes for Valentine's Day, try shamrocks for St. Patrick's Day, egg shapes for Easter, flower shapes for May Day or tree shapes for Christmas.

Button Border

Materials: Various colors and shapes of buttons; construction paper; glue; pair of scissors.

Preparation: Cut sheets of construction paper in half lengthwise to make 4½- by 12-inch strips.

Activity: Give each child a strip of construction paper and an assortment of buttons. Let the children glue their buttons on their paper strips.

Border: Attach the button-covered strips around the edges of a bulletin board.

Variation: Instead of buttons, use other materials such as small seashells, glitter or pieces of yarn.

Tube Border

Materials: Cardboard toilet tissue tubes; clothespins; red, yellow and blue tempera paint; paint brushes; shallow containers.

Preparation: Clip a clothespin on one end of each toilet tissue tube. Pour each color of tempera paint into a separate container.

Activity: Give the children the toilet tissue tubes and paint brushes. Have each child hold his or her tube by the clothespin and paint it one of the three colors. Allow the paint to dry.

Border: Attach the colorful tubes along the edges of a bulletin board, making a pattern with the colors, if possible.

Mural
Patterns

Autumn Leaves Mural Pattern

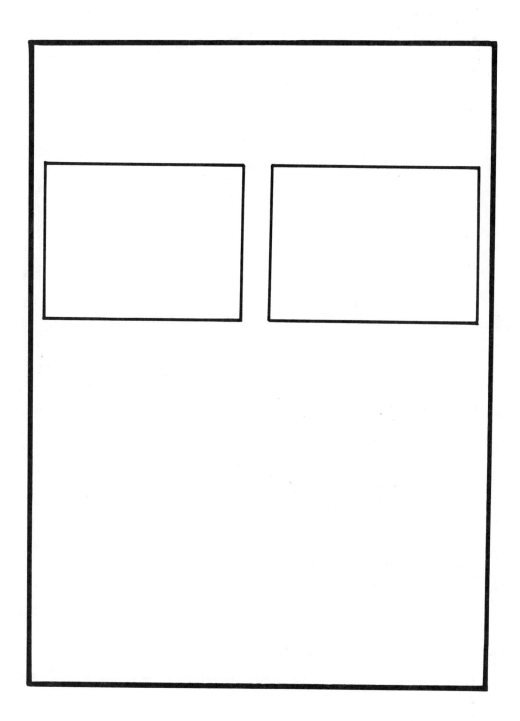

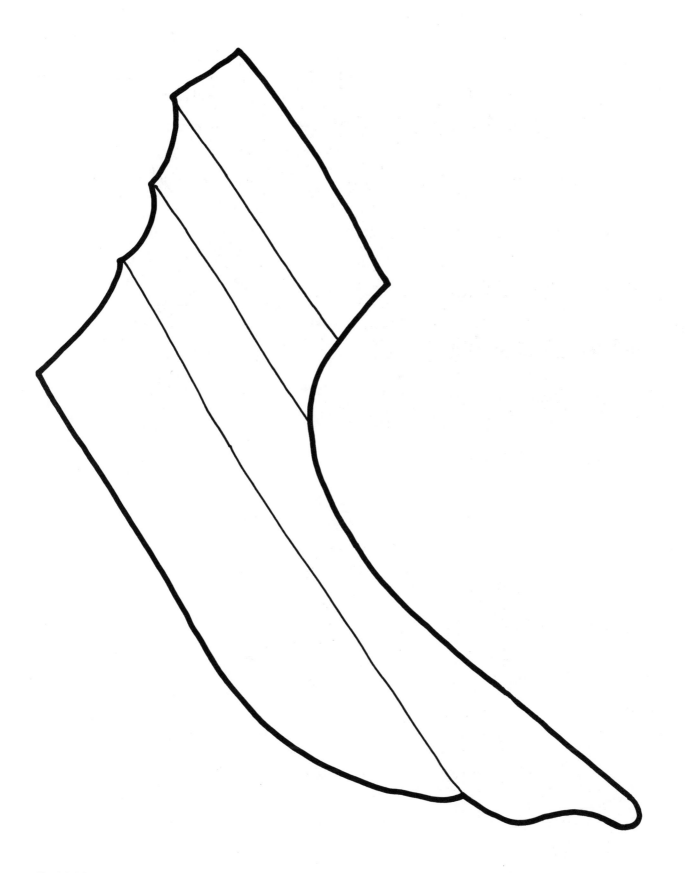

Columbus Day Mural Pattern **65**

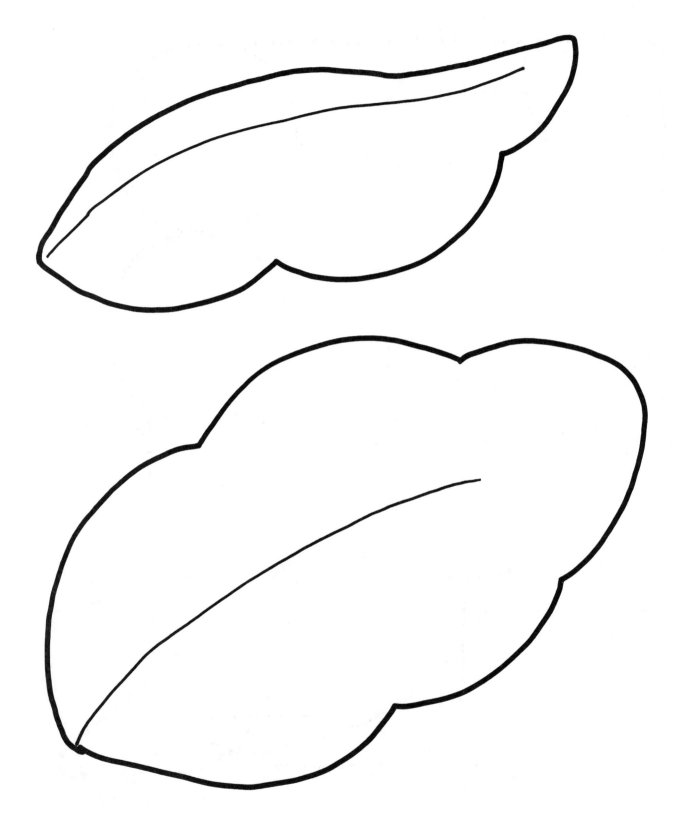

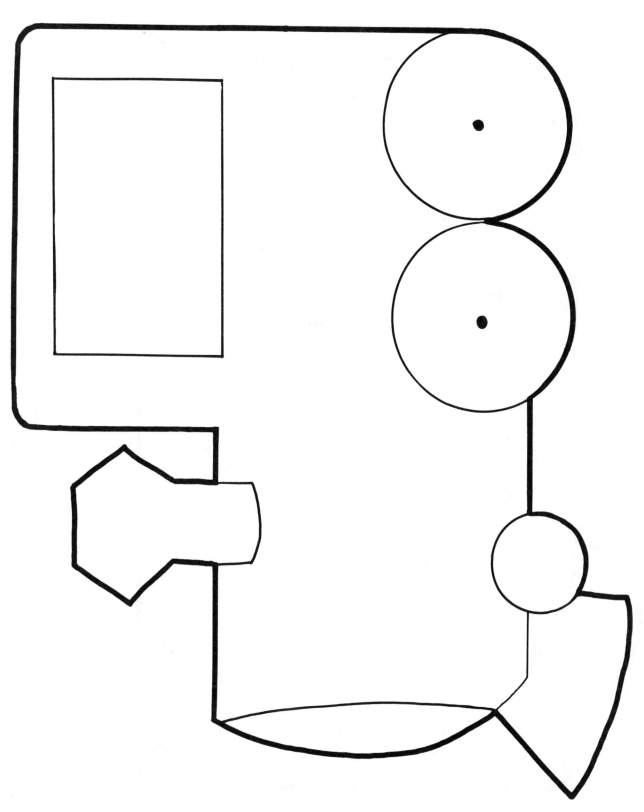

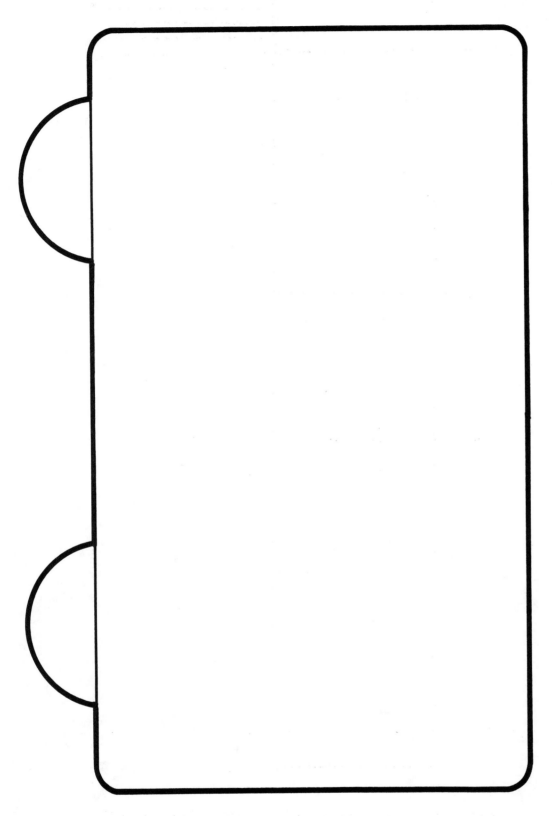

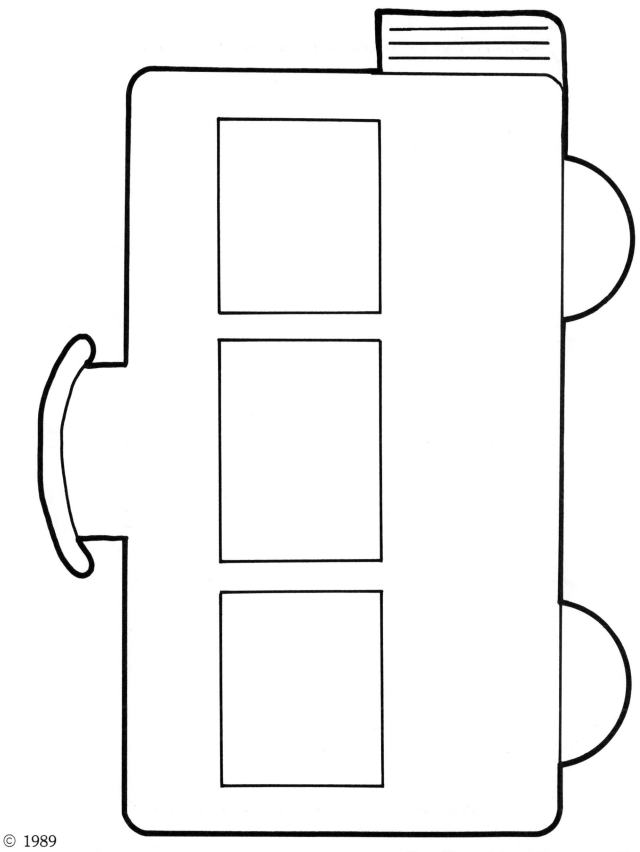

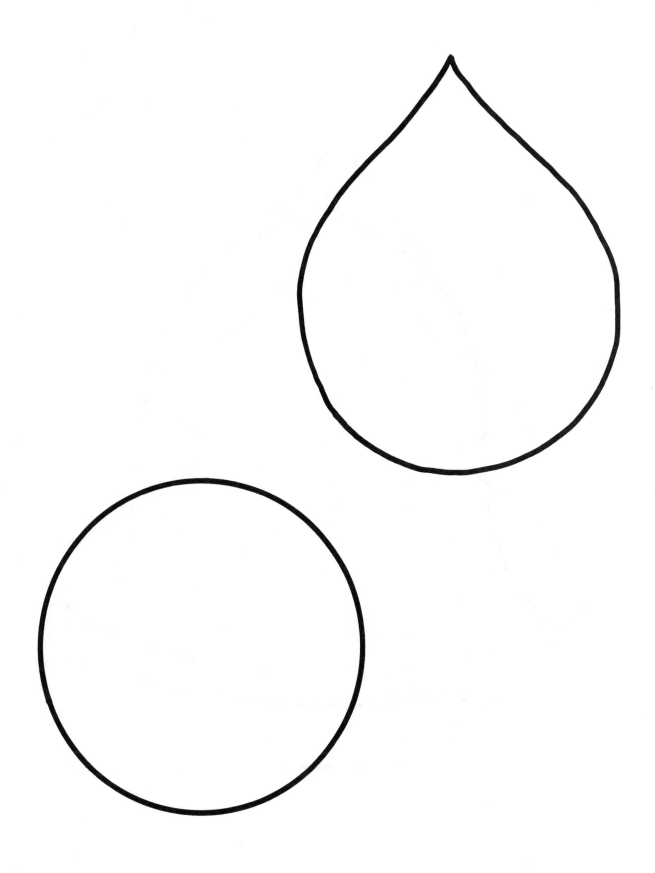

Night Sky Mural Pattern **73**

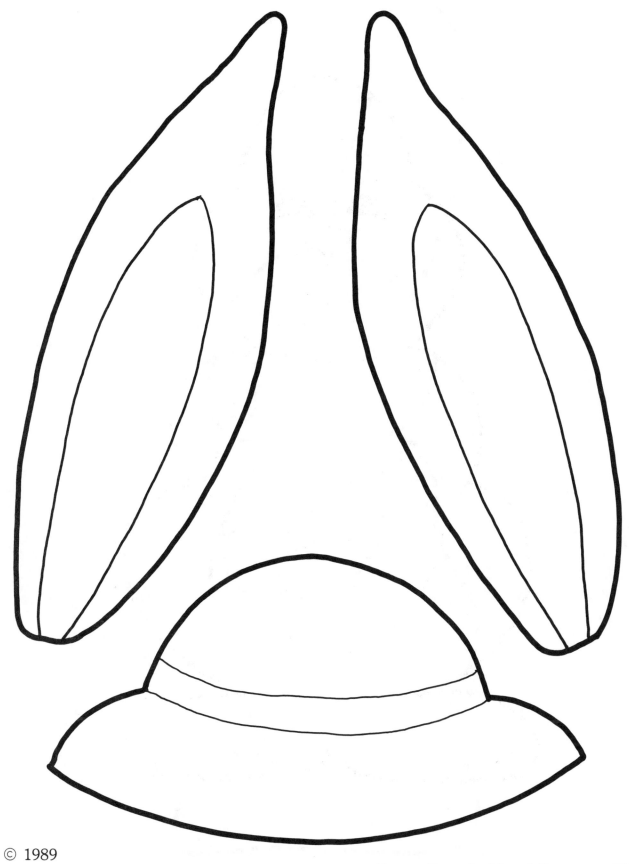

76 *Bunny Trail Mural Pattern*

© 1989
Warren Publishing House

78   *Teddy Bears' Picnic Mural Pattern*

Activity Books

BEST OF TOTLINE
Totline Magazine's best ideas.
Best of Totline Newsletter
Best of Totline Parent Flyers

BUSY BEES SERIES
Seasonal ideas for two's and three's.
Busy Bees–Fall
Busy Bees–Winter
Busy Bees–Spring
Busy Bees–Summer

CELEBRATION SERIES
Early learning through celebrations.
Small World Celebrations
Special Day Celebrations
Great Big Holiday
   Celebrations

EXPLORING SERIES
Versatile, hands-on learning.
Exploring Sand
Exploring Water
Exploring Wood

FOUR SEASONS
Active learning through the year.
Four Seasons–Art
Four Seasons–Math
Four Seasons–Movement
Four Seasons–Science

GREAT BIG THEMES SERIES
Giant units designed around a theme.
Space
Farm
Zoo
Circus

LEARNING & CARING ABOUT
Teach children about their world.
Our World
Our Selves
Our Town

PIGGYBACK SONGS
New songs sung to the tunes of childhood favorites!
Piggyback Songs
More Piggyback Songs
Piggyback Songs for
   Infants and Toddlers
Piggyback Songs in
   Praise of God
Piggyback Songs in
   Praise of Jesus
Holiday Piggyback Songs
Animal Piggyback Songs
Piggyback Songs for School
Piggyback Songs to Sign
Spanish Piggyback Songs
More Piggyback Songs
   for School

PLAY & LEARN SERIES
Learning through familiar objects.
Play & Learn with Magnets
Play & Learn with
   Rubber Stamps
Play & Learn with Photos
Play & Learn with Stickers
Play & Learn with
   Paper Shapes & Borders

1•2•3 SERIES
Open-ended learning.
1•2•3 Art
1•2•3 Games
1•2•3 Colors
1•2•3 Puppets
1•2•3 Murals
1•2•3 Books
1•2•3 Reading & Writing
1•2•3 Rhymes, Stories & Songs
1•2•3 Math
1•2•3 Science
1•2•3 Shapes

THEME-A-SAURUS SERIES
Classroom-tested, instant themes.
Theme-A-Saurus
Theme-A-Saurus II
Toddler Theme-A-Saurus
Alphabet Theme-A-Saurus
Nursery Rhyme
   Theme-A-Saurus
Storytime Theme-A-Saurus

Parent Books

A YEAR OF FUN SERIES
Age-specific books for parenting.
Just for Babies
Just for One's
Just for Two's
Just for Three's
Just for Four's
Just for Five's

BEGINNING FUN WITH ART
Introduce your child to art fun.
Beginning Fun With Scissors
Beginning Fun With Yarn

LEARNING EVERYWHERE
Discover teaching opportunities everywhere you go.
Teaching House
Teaching Trips
Teaching Town

Storytime

Delightful stories with related activity ideas, snacks, and songs.

ALPHABET & NUMBER SERIES
Kids Celebrate the Alphabet

HUFF AND PUFF SERIES
Huff and Puff's Snowy Day
Huff and Puff
   on Groundhog Day
Huff and Puff's Hat Relay
Huff and Puff's April Showers
Huff and Puff's
   Hawaiian Rainbow
Huff and Puff Go to Camp
Huff and Puff's Fourth of July
Huff and Puff Around
   the World
Huff and Puff Go to School
Huff and Puff on Halloween
Huff and Puff
   on Thanksgiving
Huff and Puff's
   Foggy Christmas

NATURE SERIES
The Bear and the Mountain
Ellie the Evergreen
The Wishing Fish

CUT & TELL CUTOUTS
Simple stories with activity ideas and cutout manipulatives.
The Gingerbread Kid
Henny Penny
The Three Bears
The Three Billy Goats Gruff
Little Red Riding Hood
The Three Little Pigs
The Big, Big Carrot
The Country Mouse and
   the City Mouse
Elves and the Shoemaker
The Hare and the Tortoise
The Little Red Hen
Stone Soup
Hickory, Dickory Dock
Humpty Dumpty
1, 2, Buckle My Shoe
Old Mother Hubbard
Rabbit, Rabbit, Carrot Eater
Twinkle, Twinkle Little Star
Cobbler, Cobbler
Hickety, Pickety
Mary, Mary, Quite Contrary
The Mulberry Bush
The Muffin Man
The Three Little Kittens

Resources

BEAR HUGS SERIES
Encourage positive attitudes.
Remembering the Rules
Staying in Line
Circle Time
Transition Times
Time Out
Saying Goodbye
Meals and Snacks
Nap Time
Cleanup
Fostering Self-Esteem
Being Afraid
Saving the Earth
Being Responsible
Getting Along
Being Healthy
Welcoming Children
Respecting Others
Accepting Change

MIX & MATCH PATTERNS
Simple patterns to save time!
Animal Patterns
Everyday Patterns
Holiday Patterns
Nature Patterns

SNACKS SERIES
Nutrition combines with learning.
Super Snacks
Healthy Snacks
Teaching Snacks
Multicultural Snacks

101 TIPS FOR DIRECTORS
Valuable tips for busy directors.
Staff and Parent Self-Esteem
Parent Communication
Health and Safety
Marketing Your Center
Resources for You
   and Your Center
Child Development Training

1001 SERIES
Super reference books.
1001 Teaching Props
1001 Teaching Tips
1001 Rhymes & Fingerplays

TEACHING PUZZLES
Kids Celebrate the Alphabet

TEACHING BORDERS
Kids Celebrate the Alphabet
Kids Celebrate Environments
Kids Celebrate the Seasons

Totline books and resources are available at parent and teacher stores. For the dealer nearest you or a catalog, call 1-800-421-5565

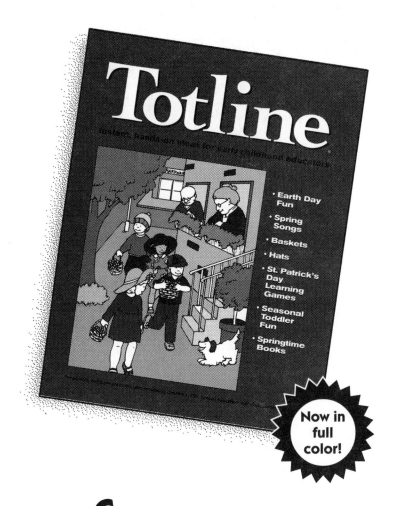

Active preschool learning— Ideas that work!

Now in full color!

* Earth Day Fun
* Spring Songs
* Baskets
* Hats
* St. Patrick's Day Learning Games
* Seasonal Toddler Fun
* Springtime Books

Challenge and engage young children with the fresh ideas for active learning in *Totline Magazine*. Developed with busy, early-childhood professionals and parents in mind, these activities need minimal preparation for successful learning fun. Each bimonthly issue is perfect for working with children ages two to six and includes • seasonal learning themes • stories, songs, and rhymes • open-ended art projects and science explorations • reproducible parent pages • ready-made teaching materials • and activites just for toddlers. *Totline Magazine* is the perfect resource for a project-based curriculum in a preschool or at home.

From Totline® Publications